I Have a Question

By Tyler Martin
Illustrated by Toby Williams

Sadlier-Oxford
A Division of William H. Sadlier, Inc.

I have a question.
What is a quail?

I have a question.
What is a queen?

I have a question.
What is a quart?

I have a question.
What is a quarter?

I have a question.
What is a quarterback?

I have a question.
What is a quartet?

Here's a quick quiz.
What other words begin
with the letters qu?